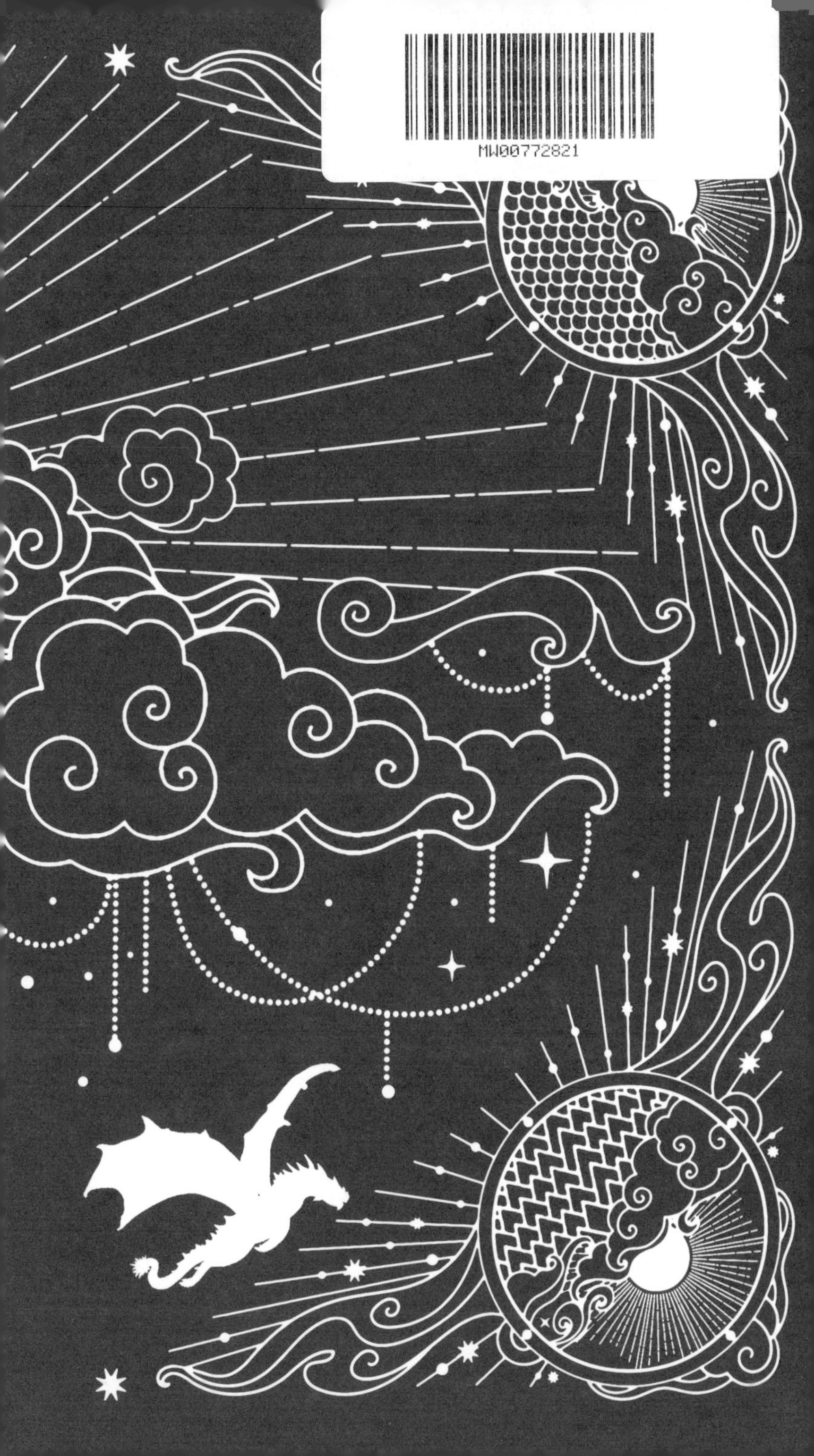

THIS JOURNAL BELONGS TO:

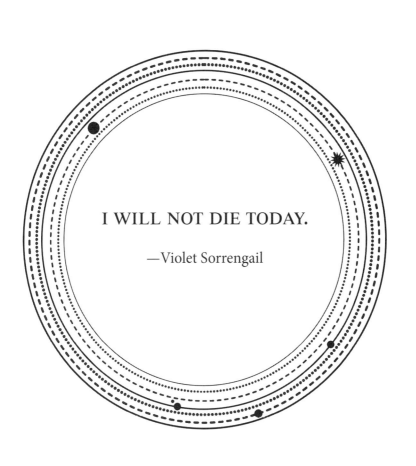

I WILL NOT DIE TODAY.

—Violet Sorrengail

I KNOW EXACTLY WHO
AND WHAT YOU ARE.

—Tairn

PLEASE DON'T MISTAKE
ANY PART OF ME FOR
SOFT OR KIND.

—Xaden Riorson

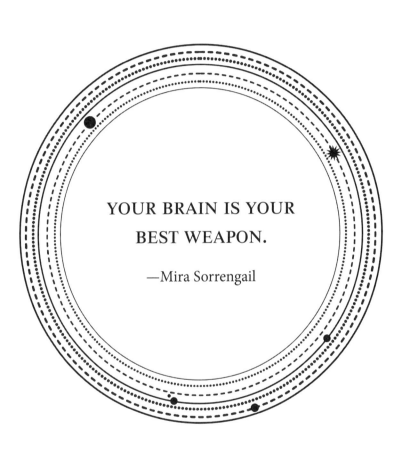

YOUR BRAIN IS YOUR
BEST WEAPON.

—Mira Sorrengail

WE'LL BE UNSTOPPABLE.

—Rhiannon Matthias

SHOULD I GET THE
WINGLEADER?

—Tairn

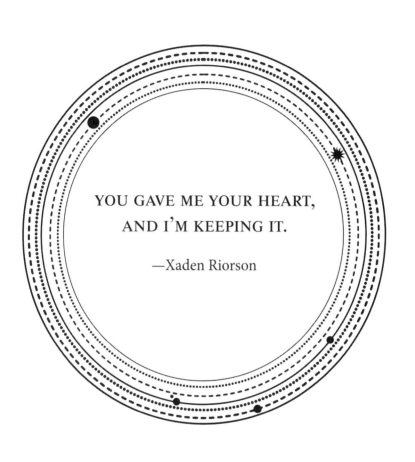

YOU GAVE ME YOUR HEART,
AND I'M KEEPING IT.

—Xaden Riorson

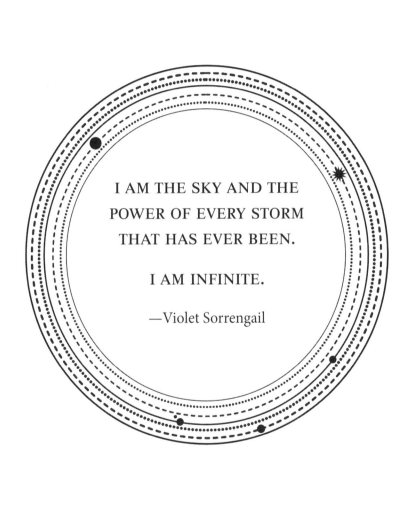

I AM THE SKY AND THE
POWER OF EVERY STORM
THAT HAS EVER BEEN.

I AM INFINITE.

—Violet Sorrengail

Official Fourth Wing Journal: Violent Little Thing Edition
Based on the novel *Fourth Wing* by Rebecca Yarros

RED TOWER
BOOKS™

ISBN 978-1-6493-7857-6
$24.99 U.S./$33.99 CAN
Manufactured in the United States of America

Cover design by Elizabeth Turner Stokes
Interior design by Britt Marczak
Stock art by FamGrafis/Shutterstock, Peratek/Shutterstock,
AlyonaZhitnaya/Shutterstock

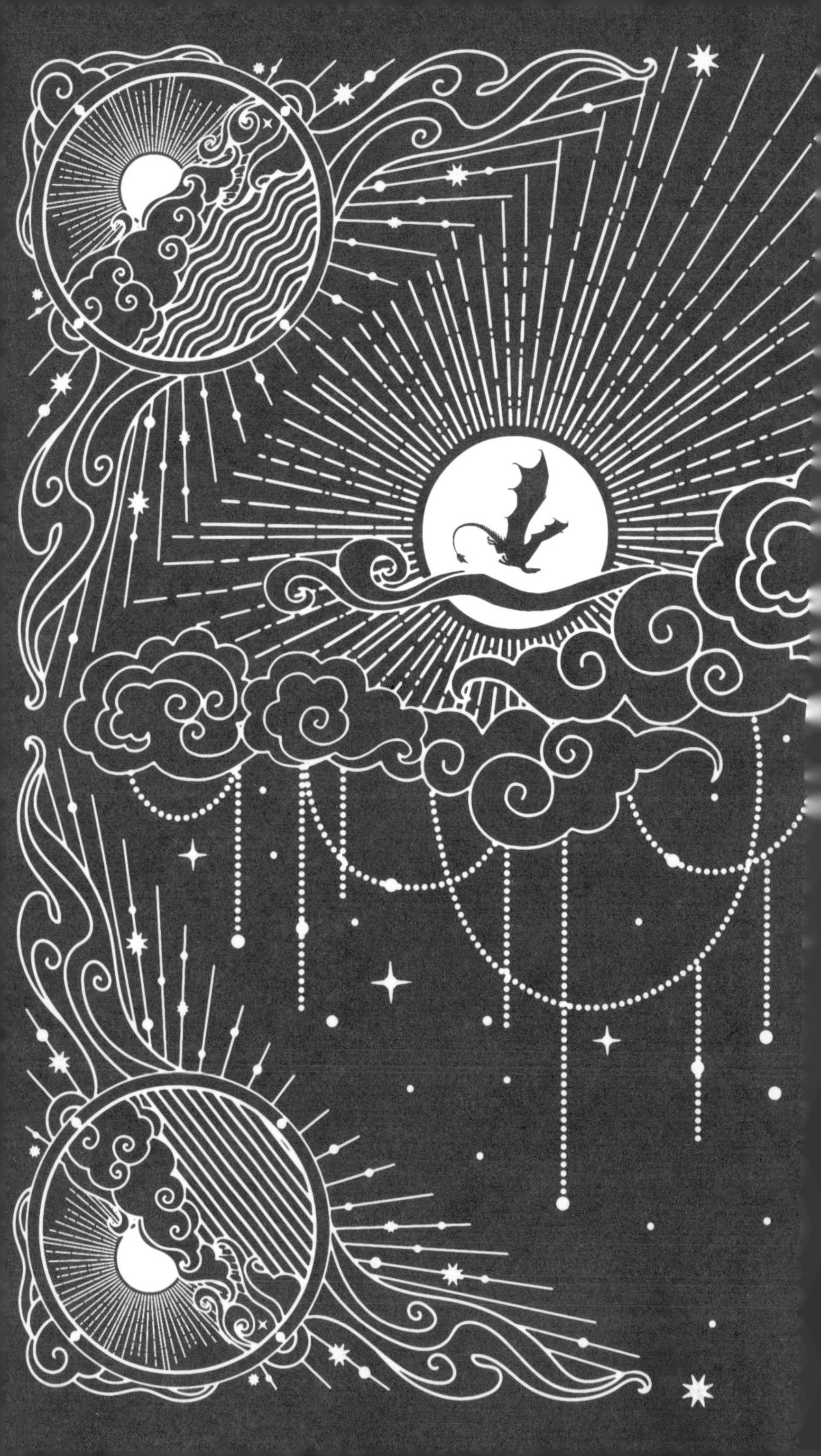